A SPECIAL THANK YOU TO MY FRIEND AND A TERRIFIC COLORIST, CHRISTY BLOUNT, FOR COLORING MY COVER AND BRINGING MY DRAWING TO LIFE.

THANK YOU FOR PURCHASING STUNNING FLOWERS ADULT COLORING BOOK. YOU CAN CHECK OUT MY OTHER COLORING BOOKS LISTED BELOW WHICH CAN BE PURCHASED AT AMAZON.COM:

VINTAGE PARIS BAKE SHOP (Adult)
VINTAGE WINE GARDEN (Adult)
ICE CREAM MADNESS (Adult)
ICE CREAM MADNESS VOLUME 2 (Adult)
TEA & COFFEE TROPICAL TREASURES (Adult)
TEA & COFFEE OCEAN TREASURES (Adult)
TEA & COFFEE TREASURES (Adult)
BOTANICAL FLOWERS & MANDALAS (Adult)
MAJESTIC FALL (Adult)
A VERY RETRO CHRISTMAS (Adult)
MAGICAL DESSERTS (Kids)
MAGICAL DESSERTS VOLUME 2 (Kids)
MAGICAL DESSERTS VOLUME 3 (Kids)
FASHION DOLLS (Adult)
FAIRIES IN THE FLOWER GARDEN (Adult)
MERMAID'S WONDERLAND SEA OF ENCHANTMENT (Adult)
CHRISTMAS DESSERTS
VALENTINE'S DAYDREAMS COLORING BOOK (Adult)
VALENTINE'S DAY DELIGHTS (Adult)
VALENTINE'S FLOWERS & DESSERTS (Adult)
VALENTINE'S DAY DESSERTS (Adult)
VALENTINE'S DAY ANIMALS & Sweets (Kids)
VALENTINE DAY'S FLOWERS (Adult)
A VERY RUSTIC VALENTINE'S DAY (Adult)
ELEGANT FLOWERS (Adult)
ST. PATRICK'S DAY BLESSINGS (Adult)
A HAPPY ST. PATTY'S DAY (Kids)
ST. PATRICK'S DAY DESSERTS (Adult)
ST. PATRICK DAY FLOWERS (Adult)
SPRINGTIME FAIRIES (Adult)
SPECTACULAR DESSERTS (Adult)
BEAUTIFUL SPRINGTIME FLOWERS (Adult)
MERMAID DESSERTS (Adult)
FLORAL DELIGHTS (Adult)
FABULOUS SPRINGTIME WREATHS (Adult)
DELICIOUS SPRINGTIME DESSERTS (Adult)
CHARMING EASTER FLOWERS (Adult)
EASTER WONDERLAND (Adult)
EASTER BLESSINGS (Adult)
LOVELY EASTER WREATHS (Adult)
EASTER BASKETS (Adult)
(Continued on next page)
GORGEOUS SPRINGTIME FLOWERS (Adult)
MARVELOUS SPRINGTIME FLOWERS (Adult)
MAGNIFICENT FLOWERS (Adult)
AMAZING FLOWERS (Adult)

CHEERFUL FLOWERS (Adult)
LOVELY FLOWERS (Adult)
PRECIOUS FLOWERS (Adult)

IF YOU ENJOYED YOUR COLORING EXPERIENCE, PLEASE TELL OTHERS ABOUT IT BY WRITING A REVIEW ON AMAZON.COM UNDER THE B